FOREWORD

The triangular-shaped street pattern of Chapel Street, Greengate and Gravel Lane formed the heart of the medieval town and is one of the few physical reminders of Salford's historic core that is still visible in the modern cityscape. Salford's early development has been the subject of previous volumes in the *Greater Manchester's Past Revealed* series, based largely on archaeological excavations along Greengate. The fresh insight into life in medieval and post-medieval Salford gained from these previous excavations has been enhanced by the extensive archaeological work carried out between 2005 and 2016 in advance of the Chapel Wharf development, situated on the fringe of the medieval town. These excavations furnished significant new evidence for the evolution of the historic settlement, and yielded one of the largest assemblages of post-medieval pottery to have ever been recovered from the city. The excavations also highlighted the important role Salford played in the industrialisation of the region. In particular, Chapel Wharf was occupied from 1799 by one of the first iron-framed buildings in the world, which was erected as an expansion to the famous Salford Twist Mill. In addition, in 1806 the mill became the first in the world to have been lit by gas. The mill's gas plant was also used to illuminate several lights on Chapel Street, making this the earliest street known to have been lit by gas. This lavishly illustrated booklet sets out the fascinating and significant discoveries made during the excavations at Chapel Wharf, and makes an important addition to the existing portfolio of publications dedicated to historic Salford.

CONTEN[TS]

IAN MILLER
COUNTY ARCHAEOLOGIST
GREATER MANCHESTER ARCHAEOLOGICAL ADVISORY SERVICE

GMAAS
Greater Manchester Archaeological Advisory Service

Chapel Street is one of Salford's most ancient thoroughfares. It has seen centuries of development culminating in the industrial period, when every available parcel of land was built upon for industrial, commercial or domestic use. By the late 20th century many of these near-redundant structures merely echoed their industrial past, while others had been completely devastated by air strikes during the Second World War. Several regeneration projects began transforming former industrial sites in the historic core of Salford into modern facilities, attracting both vibrant new

Aerial view of Phase 2 excavation of workers' housing on Clowes Street, 2007 (© University of Manchester Archaeological Unit)

communities and visitors. Numerous schemes have targeted vacant plots along Chapel Street, creating a refurbished gateway into the city centre; the results of archaeological excavations and historic building surveys undertaken as part of these schemes are presented in *Greater Manchester's Past Revealed 27*.

Another major scheme, sited on the periphery of the former medieval heart of Salford, is at Chapel Wharf, a 4.4 acre (1.78 hectare) plot of land between Chapel Street and the River Irwell. The Chapel Wharf development consists of four towers, between 12 and 22 storeys high, which will see almost 1000 one-, two- and three-bedroom apartments, along with new public areas and walkways. The venture was set in motion in 1994, financed by Dandara Limited, and has been delivered by Sir Robert McAlpine. The scheme is just one aspect of major plans for Chapel Street, including the Chapel Wharf Development Framework, adopted by Salford City Council in 2022, to bring new homes, hotels, shops, restaurants and around 11,000 jobs to a prime city location.

Following an initial consultation with the Greater Manchester Archaeological Advisory Service (GMAAS), archaeological considerations were addressed at an early stage in the design process. Initially, a desk-top study was prepared, concluding that the site had high potential to contain remains of local and potentially of national archaeological interest spanning the medieval to industrial periods. To mitigate the harm to or loss of archaeological remains, GMAAS recommended that further investigations were warranted in the form of three phases of evaluation and excavation in specifically targeted areas across the site. Archaeological investigations were conducted from June 2005 until September 2016.

In advance of the new development, Dandara Limited commissioned the University of Manchester Archaeological Unit in 2005–07 to undertake the first and second phases of work, followed by trial trenching carried out by Oxford Archaeology North in 2014, while Salford Archaeology completed the final phase of works in 2016. The excavations uncovered a wealth of archaeological remains including medieval burgage boundaries, late 18th- and early 19th-century workers' houses, domestic-based workshops and the basement of the Salford Twist Mill, with surviving elements of the original power systems and the mill's innovative fireproof frame. The generous funding provided by Dandara Limited has enabled Salford Archaeology to explore several avenues of research based on the extraordinary finds from the excavation, dating from the 13th to 20th centuries.

Boundary ditch cut through medieval plough soil excavated during the Phase 2 evaluation and excavation at Clowes Street, 2007 (©University of Manchester Archaeological Unit)

Salford grew as a medieval settlement strategically positioned in a bend on the River Irwell, which provided an abundance of natural resources as well as protection. The town developed around the two main thoroughfares, Chapel Street and Greengate, which were linked by Gravel Lane to form a triangular route around the historic core. Salford was established as an official town being granted market status by Henry III in 1228, whilst in 1230, Ranulph de Blundeville, Earl of Chester, granted the settlement its Borough Charter.

The earliest map of Salford dates to *c.*1650 and shows the growth of the town with Sacred Trinity Church, built in *c.*1635, depicted at the junction of Gravel Lane and Chapel Street. Several burgage plots are captured on the mapping along Greengate and Chapel Street. These small plots of land were rented by the people who lived in the town. Chapel Wharf was located on the fringe of the medieval settlement and the burgage plots can be seen to stop there, with much of the site lying in open fields.

Sacred Trinity Church in the 19th century, to the north-east of Chapel Wharf (courtesy of Digital Salford)

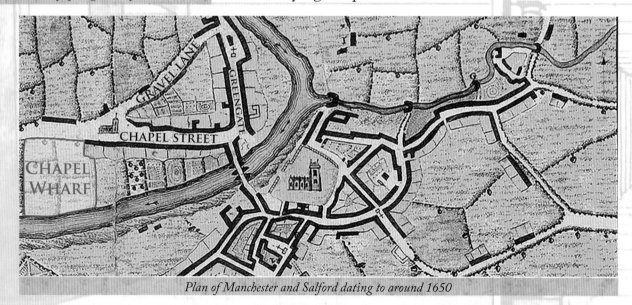

Plan of Manchester and Salford dating to around 1650

Agriculture was the main source of Salford's economy during the post-medieval period, although this was increasingly supplemented by the weaving of traditional textiles like woollen cloth, linen and fustian in domestic-based workshops, giving rise to weavers' cottages. These cottages developed into three-storey terraced dwellings in the 18th century. The third storey, known as a loomshop, was where weaving took place. A loomshop needed good daylight, controlled ventilation, heat and storage. They can often be identified by the presence of a long window of multiple lights in the upper storey, which provided sufficient daylight to operate a loom.

Development along Chapel Street extended westwards during the 18th century. Cartographers Casson and Berry captured the expansion of Salford on their map of 1745, which shows buildings encroaching into the area of the Chapel Wharf development, along the Chapel Street frontage. Surviving to the north-west of the site were the remains of two 18th-century weavers' cottages, with blocked-up long, narrow windows. Although these buildings were outside the development area, they give an insight into the former character of the Chapel Street area at the dawn of industrialisation.

Weavers' cottages fronting Chapel Street and Phase 2 excavation area along Clowes Street in 2007
(© University of Manchester Archaeological Unit)

The onset of industrialisation saw the transition from domestic workshops to a factory-based system, facilitated by the mechanisation of the cotton and woollen spinning industries that enabled goods to be produced on an unprecedented scale. New factories created numerous employment opportunities, attracting people from the country to settle in the rapidly expanding towns. The cotton industry – based on imported raw materials – dominated Lancashire's economy from the 18th century. The urgent imperative to transport both raw and manufactured bulk goods prompted the construction of the national canal network, inspired by the success of Britain's first industrial canal, the Duke of Bridgewater's Canal, built in 1761 and completed to Manchester in 1764–65.

The semi-rural landscape of Salford was replaced by a network of formally laid streets, accommodating a huge number of workers' houses plus industrial and commercial premises that were needed to meet the demands of the rapidly expanding population, trade and industry. William Green's map of Manchester and Salford, dating to 1787–94, best captures the effects of industrialisation, showing densely packed workers' housing interspersed with small workshops and large factories at Chapel Wharf. By the turn of the century, one of the last vacant parcels of land was developed into the Salford Twist Mill. Aerial photographs taken in the 20th century show the colossal size of the former Twist Mill (taken over by

Aerial photograph of Chapel Wharf in 1938, showing the former mill (© Britain From Above & Historic England)

Manchester Bonded Warehouse Company in 1844), which would have towered above, and polluted, neighbouring dwellings with coal smoke.

Throughout the 19th century, the poorest working people lived in squalor without any basic sanitary facilities and in overcrowded small dwellings. A number of successive housing reforms sought to improve living conditions for the working people. By the 20th century, some of the worst slums had begun to be demolished. At Chapel Wharf, several dilapidated streets to the south-west of the former Twist Mill were demolished by 1908 and the land was redeveloped into a finishing works, and a publishing and printing works. Dwellings on the north-east side of the mill, at Barlow's Croft and Chapel Street,

Houses in Salford during the 1950s
(courtesy of Manchester Local Image Collection)

continued to be inhabited, but were in a ruinous condition. The former mill buildings continued to function as a bonded warehouse until the Second World War, when incendiary bombs razed the building to the ground during the Manchester Blitz of 1940–41. An array of warehouses was built on the site in the mid-20th century, but these had gone out of use towards the end of the century.

The current wave of regeneration in Salford began in the late 20th century and the area has since seen a huge amount of investment, with a focus on providing new homes. The archaeological investigations undertaken prior to the development at Chapel Wharf have provided an insight into Salford's changing townscape from a small town in the 13th century into a major industrial centre in the 19th century. The excavations have also provided an invaluable opportunity to investigate a plot of land that was situated on the fringe of the medieval settlement, which otherwise has few surviving physical remains. It also gives archaeologists a chance to research the changing social structure within the heart of Salford as the town underwent intense industrialisation.

Prehistoric activity has been detected on higher, well-drained land on the opposite side of the River Irwell to Chapel Wharf, with concentrations of artefacts discovered in two locations: Castlefield, where Mesolithic (*c.*10,000 BC to *c.*4000 BC) to Bronze Age (*c.*2300 BC to 700 BC) stone tools were discovered and Bronze Age or Iron Age (*c.*700 BC to AD 43) pottery have been found; and in the vicinity of Manchester Cathedral, where the ritual deposition of metalwork took place during the Bronze Age.

Less prehistoric activity has been identified on the lower-lying marshy terrain on the western side of the River Irwell, in the area now known as Salford. During the 19th century, antiquarians came across several potential Neolithic stone tools south-west of Chapel Wharf. More recently, a fragment of worked flint was recovered during an excavation in the centre of Salford at One Greengate.

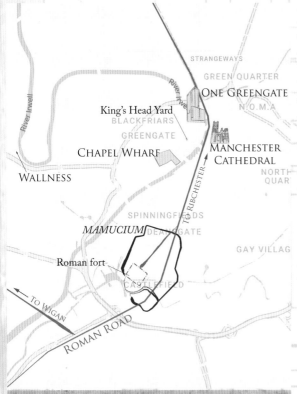

Plan showing the locations of places mentioned in the text (© Google)

A few abraded fragments of Roman pottery were also recovered from the One Greengate excavation, whilst a Roman tile was found during an excavation of King's Head Yard on Chapel Street. Nevertheless, the focus of Roman occupation in the area was on the Manchester side of the River Irwell where a fort, known as *Mamucium,* was constructed from earth and timber in the late 1st century AD. Beyond the fort, which was rebuilt in stone in *c.*AD 200, archaeological investigations have uncovered the remains of a substantial *vicus* or civilian settlement that was occupied until the early 3rd century AD. A network of roads linked *Mamucium* to Ribchester in the north and Wigan in the west, along with connections to Chester, Castleshaw and Buxton. The road to Wigan took a course across the River Irwell and through Salford, and was reportedly still visible as an earthwork in the 19th century.

The fall of the Western Roman Empire in the 5th century AD saw the collapse of centralised authority in Britain, with the abandonment of many of the established settlements and forts. As the Romans withdrew, Germanic and Danish tribes took advantage of this opportunity and began first to raid Britain and then to settle in areas throughout the island. After centuries of mass migrations, new identities, cultures and boundaries were forged, roughly corresponding with those still in existence today. In the 5th century, tradition states that town defences were created in Wallness, when Germanus, the Bishop of Auxerre, accompanied by St. Patrick, visited Britain to repel Pelagian heresy. The record of their journey suggests that they were refused access to a walled city, and instead

John Speed's map of 1610, showing Salford Hundred

encamped on the banks of *Gidea Broc*, a stream that runs through Salford. The 'walled city' seems likely to have been the fortified city of Salford 'with its great ramparts at *Waellraess*'.

According to the Anglo-Saxon Chronicle, Salford was part of the kingdom of Northumbria until Edward the Elder conquered the area in AD 923. During this time, it is likely that a settlement grew at Salford, taking its name from the Anglo-Saxon word *Sealhford* meaning 'ford by the willows'. The crossing point may have been situated immediately upstream of the medieval Salford Bridge, at the junction of Greengate and Chapel Street. An Anglo-Saxon royal manor with a royal hall may have occupied a position close to the ancient ford, on the site of the later Salford Hall.

Salford's importance as the head of a hundred, a vast administrative centre, had been established before the Norman Conquest of 1066. Salford Hundred comprised 11 parishes stretching from Rossendale Valley in the north to the River Mersey in the south and partially followed the course of the River Tame in the east. The earliest description of Salford Hundred is in the Domesday Survey of 1086, recording that Edward the Confessor, one of the last Anglo-Saxon kings of England, held the manor before William the Conqueror granted the land to Roger de Poitou. By this time, the Salford Hundred covered an area of 350 square miles, with a population believed to have totalled around 35,000.

Early in the 13th century, a small town began to emerge at Salford, which was positioned strategically in a bend of the River Irwell. The town was centred around its two main streets, Greengate and Chapel Street (known formerly as Sergeant Street), which met at the historic fording point that crossed into the neighbouring settlement of Manchester. Gravel Lane linked the two streets at a slightly later date, forming a triangular tract of land. The surrounding farmland and pastures were suitable for growing oats, wheat, barley and beans, forming the foundations for Salford's economy. Salford's booming economy is reflected in Henry III's decision to grant the town market status and the right to hold an annual fair in 1228.

By 1230 Ranulf de Blundeville, Earl of Chester, had granted the charter by which the town became a free borough. The burgesses – the new freemen of the borough – had certain privileges over traders living outside Salford, such as being exempt from paying tolls at markets and fairs. In addition, a borough court was established in the centre of the market place that was built exclusively for the use of the burgesses, and was distinct from the lord's feudal court. Salford's position as a free borough motivated several prominent families to move to the area, and by the late medieval period Salford had over 30 manors within a five-mile radius.

Ranulf de Blundeville

Extract from Casson and Berry's plan of Salford and Manchester in 1745

The introduction of the burgage system to Salford in the 13th century saw the open manorial fields divided up into narrow tracts of land known as burgage plots, which were allotted by the lord of the manor to the town's burgesses. Rather than giving service to the manor, as a freeman would under the former feudal system, a burgess was obliged to pay a fixed annual monetary rent. The obligation on the burgesses to pay rent compelled them to become entrepreneurs and often burgages were subdivided to form smaller plots that could be rented out. It was this dynamic, along with the burgesses' right to vote in town elections, that led Salford to develop into a thriving trading centre.

Extract from Casson and Berry's plan of 1745, showing Salford

Typically, burgages were fronted by a dwelling, with an elongated rear plot used for agricultural purposes or for various small-scale industries. In 1346 Salford had 129 burgages owned by 52 individuals, suggesting that the town had a population of between 200 and 300 people. A number of property boundaries are shown on the earliest plan of Salford and Manchester dating to *c*.1650, and also on Casson and Berry's more detailed plan of 1745. Evidence for possible medieval burgage ditches, which demarcated the plots, has been recorded on the northern side of Greengate, to the north-east of Chapel Wharf.

A few artefacts and features pertaining to the medieval period have been discovered across the historic core of Salford. Most notably, at the junction of Greengate and Gravel Lane two large rubbish pits were found containing 13th- and 14th-century pottery, and an archer's brace made from the sole of a leather shoe. The remains of a possible medieval bakehouse were also exposed on the site of the former Exchange Railway Station to the north-east of Chapel Wharf.

In most cases, the medieval pottery from the Chapel Wharf excavation, which is very fragmentary, was found in later plough soils or ditches. The pottery was probably mixed together with manure and other household waste that was used to fertilise the open fields that once covered the site.

Jar body sherd with clear glaze. 13th–14th centur

Pottery known as northern gritty ware characterises the local ceramic tradition between the late 11th and early 13th centuries, with partially reduced wares becoming prevalent by the late 13th century. Most medieval pot from Greater Manchester seems to be derived from coal measure clays, which are found throughout Lancashire, parts of Cheshire, and West and South Yorkshire. No kiln sites have been identified in Greater Manchester, which appears to be a melting pot for medieval ceramic traditions. Some medieval ceramics found in Salford are comparable to those found at Norton Priory in Cheshire, whilst some pottery from Ordsall Hall,

14th-century olive-green glazed body sherd exterior sooting

Salford, has stylistic analogies to traditions found in Doncaster. South-east of Manchester, the medieval ceramic repertoire from Mellor, for instance, has affinities with West Yorkshire and Derbyshire traditions more than south-west Lancashire.

Medieval potters were generally quite limited in the range of vessels they produced, with jar and jug forms being the most common. These were pots used to store food or liquid, or in the case of some of the jars, telltale sooting indicates that they were used to cook food.

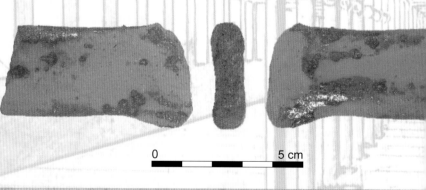

Fragment of a strap handle from a 14th-century jug

A layer of medieval soil was truncated in the centre of the 2007 evaluation area by a series of ditches and a stone wall probably dating to the early post-medieval period. In the north-eastern part of the evaluation area, a ditch with a north-west by south-east orientation was found to contain ceramics from the 17th and 18th centuries. To the south of this, with a perpendicular orientation, was another ditch also containing post-medieval pottery. These ditches likely demarcated boundaries connected to properties fronting Chapel Street or the edges of fields extending south-eastwards to the river. Just over a metre to the west of the north-east by south-west orientated ditch was a stone wall. As there were no associated floor surfaces, and because post-medieval horticultural layers had built up around it, the wall was also interpreted as a post-medieval boundary marker.

The earliest surviving structural remains at Chapel Wharf – comprising two roughly built sandstone walls – were found beneath a late 18th-century dwelling and post-medieval garden soil. No mortar was visible between the stonework of the wall, which had a rough, unshaped appearance consistent with a medieval or early post-medieval date. It has been suggested that the stone wall may have marked the original boundary of medieval Salford.

Post-medieval ditch running along the south-west side of Clowes Street in 2007
(© University of Manchester Archaeological Unit)

The remains of a second ditch running beneath the access for Salford Twist Mill in 2007
(© University of Manchester Archaeological Unit)

An early stone wall excavated in 2007
(© University of Manchester Archaeological Unit)

Midlands Purple-type earthenware

The site yielded many sherds of pottery that demonstrate Salford's continuing development as a commercial hub throughout the post-medieval period. An assemblage of pottery found in a ditch at Chapel Wharf was probably refuse from the beer house that is believed to have stood on the site in the 17th century and later became the Lord Nelson Inn. Interestingly, a deposit containing similar ceramic material has been recently excavated nearby on the site of the former King's Head Inn, on the other side of Chapel Street.

Multi-handled drinking cup or tyg, dating to the 17th century

Although some sherds of potentially 14th- or 15th-century Cistercian ware cups were found, much of the pottery assemblage was composed of dark-glazed or Midlands Purple-type earthenwares. It has been suggested that the dark glazing reflects the 17th-century Puritan fashion for dark, sombre clothing.

Some of the most striking vessels to be found during the excavation were luxury ceramics, including 17th- to early 18th-century dark-glazed fine wares such as near-complete multi-handled drinking cups, as well as fragments of candlesticks, a chafing dish (a kind of early camping stove used either to cook food or keep it warm, using charcoal as fuel), and possible chamber pots.

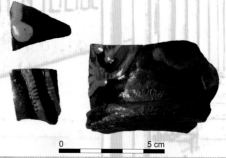

Sherds of glazed Cistercian ware cups

Contrasting with the drab nature of dark-glazed earthenwares, slipwares perhaps appear as ceramic responses to the restoration of the monarchy after the Commonwealth period. With their bright yellows or oranges and contrasting slip-trailed decoration, they have an enduring attraction that continues to the present day.

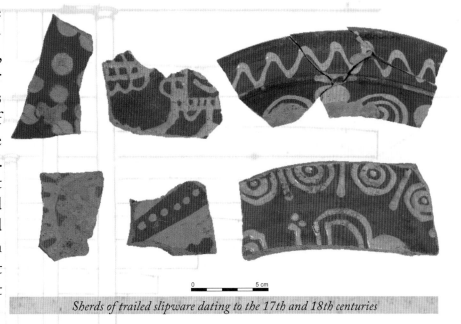

Sherds of trailed slipware dating to the 17th and 18th centuries

Although only making up a small proportion of the pottery found at Chapel Wharf, the slipwares more than make up for this deficit by the skill and imagination that went into the vessels found on the site. The range of vessels includes slip-trailed dishes similar to examples dating to *c*.1690 from Burslem, Staffordshire, as well as the rounded body of a jug or jar with feathered decoration, also reminiscent of similarly dated vessels from Staffordshire. Also present were fragments of press-moulded plates with piecrust rims and cup fragments with simple trailed spots. Despite Staffordshire being closely associated with slipwares, such wares were manufactured at many sites across Britain, with a site investigated at Lazencroft near Leeds (West

Sherds of Staffordshire-type slipware

Yorkshire) and a site on the Cumbrian coast both producing similar wares. Good examples of slipware were also found during recent excavations in Prescot. The slipwares from the excavations may have been produced locally, although firm evidence for pottery kilns in Salford and Manchester has yet to be discovered.

Casson and Berry's map of 1745 not only records aspects of Salford's historic rural landscape, but also captures the expansion of the town along the Greengate and Chapel Street frontages. The first development within the Chapel Wharf site comprised a long narrow range of buildings situated to the east. This range ended in a block of four dwellings built around a square central courtyard. To the rear of the properties were small enclosed rectangular plots, presumably delineating kitchen gardens or orchards.

Manchester panorama 1760 (© Manchester Archives)

Before industrialisation, agricultural products had formed the foundation of Salford's economy, but as the post-medieval period progressed so did the importance of small-scale cottage industries such as clogging, cobbling, brewing and weaving. Textile processing in particular increased throughout the 16th century, leading to the development of a distinctive kind of production site, the weavers' cottage. Weavers' cottages were designed to facilitate the weaving of woollen cloth, linen and fustian in the well-lit upper storey of a domestic dwelling. Merchants supplied raw materials to the weavers' cottages that were in turn woven into cloth using handlooms. The finished products were traded at Greengate cloth hall in Salford.

The economic importance of textile processing increased significantly throughout the 17th century, prompted by the importation of cotton to south-east Lancashire from the first half of the 17th century. In the uplands to the east and north of Manchester, the fast- and strong- flowing streams provided ideal conditions for merchants, landowners and tenant farmers to set up water-powered mills, augmenting the profusion of vernacular workshops already found amongst the steep-sided valleys.

By the late 18th century, as textile spinning became increasingly mechanised, the factory system began to replace domestic-based cottage industries, causing drastic cultural, social and economic changes. During this time, although Salford was urbanising, it did not evolve into the same kind of commercial centre as Manchester, but retained its role as a regional distribution centre for traditional textiles.

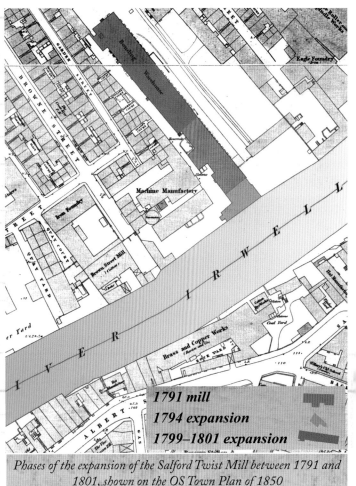

1791 mill
1794 expansion
1799–1801 expansion

Phases of the expansion of the Salford Twist Mill between 1791 and 1801, shown on the OS Town Plan of 1850

The booming textile trade relied heavily on the transportation of both raw and finished products. Originally, goods were delivered by road using pack animals and carts. However, this method was more expensive and inefficient relative to new forms of transport. Water transportation allowed the movement of large cargoes of goods. The Mersey & Irwell Navigation Company was founded in 1721, aspiring to create a navigable route from Liverpool to Salford and Manchester. Work began in 1724 and required the construction of eight locks between Manchester and Warrington, beyond which the River Mersey was tidal. The navigation was completed in around 1734, opening up trade to Salford and Manchester from the expanding port of Liverpool.

Casson & Berry's 1745 plan of Manchester and Salford shows the development of a 'kay' on the south side of the River Irwell in Manchester. Edward Byrom, a wealthy fustian dealer and one of the proprietors of the Mersey & Irwell Navigation Company, built the quay and associated warehouses in 1735. The quay had a river frontage of 136 yards and had wharfage facilities for boats of up to 50 tons. In order to secure trade with Salford, a second quay was built on the opposite side of the Irwell in 1755, connected to Chapel Street by Quay Street.

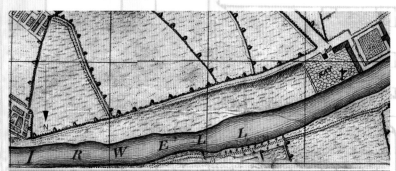

Extract from Casson and Berry's plan of 1745, showing the 'kay' on the south bank of the River Irwell

As the 18th century progressed, so too did technological innovations, which saw the replacement of water-powered mills with steam. The advent of the steam engine hugely benefited Salford, which had very few sites suitable for water-powered factories, largely because the mature state of the River Irwell did not provide a strong enough flow of water to power a waterwheel. The town's earliest mills were thus built on the fringe of the urban area, upstream at Pendleton and Kersal. In Pendleton, William Douglas established one of Lancashire's earliest water-powered mills in 1782. Another early water-powered mill was opened in the same year by the partnership of Ackers, Beever & Co on the River Irwell at Broken Bank, to the west of Salford's historic core.

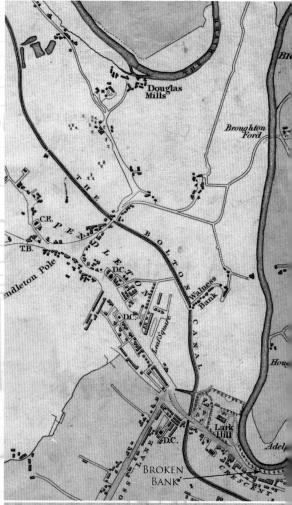

Douglas Mills, built just to the north of Pendleton. Broke Bank is situated just north of The Crescent (Johnson, 182¢

The introduction of steam power to drive textile machinery in the late 1780s enabled entrepreneurs to build factories in the centre of Salford and Manchester where, due to the expansion of the canal network, coal was readily available. Green's plan of Manchester and Salford, dating to 1787–94, shows the location of Salford Quay immediately to the south-west of Chapel Wharf, a desirable location for the first steam-powered cotton mill in Salford, known as Salford Twist Mill. The factory was built in 1791 on a plot of land owned by Salford Company and originally comprised a small rectangular range, aligned north-west/south-east, on the banks of the River Irwell. This was to become one of the most sophisticated and innovative 18th-century industrial complexes in the world.

Green's plan of Manchester and Salford, dating to 1787–94, showing Chapel Wharf and the immediate environs

The mill at Chapel Wharf was established by the Salford Twist or Engine Twist Company. The original mill building, shown on Green's map, was a seven-storey structure with an engine house situated at the southern end of the mill housing a substantial 30hp steam engine, an enormous capacity for the time.

Cotton yarn was produced in the mill using Arkwright water frames, patented in 1769 by early industrial pioneer, Richard Arkwright. The spinning frame was originally a water-powered machine that produced strong twisted threads of yarn by using wooden and metal cylinders that span multiple threads of yarn at the same time. Experienced workers were not required to operate the new machinery, replacing a process that had been done for centuries by skilled hands. The introduction of the mechanised carding engine in 1775 to supply the spinning frames was fundamental to the inauguration of the factory system. The net result of mechanising the initial processing and subsequent spinning of cotton was a great reduction in the cost of cotton yarn.

Original spinning machine, Sir Richard Arkwright and John Kay, England, 1769 (© The Board of Trustees of the Science Museum)

Samuel Crompton, a Bolton-born inventor who as a child spun yarn with a spinning jenny, created the spinning mule between 1775 and 1779. This device was a cross between Arkwright's water frame and the spinning jenny. The spinning mule made it possible to produce high-quality thread for the textile industry on a wide scale. The spinning mule's design was not patented, allowing other engineers to modify it to increase efficiency. For example, unlike Crompton's machine, mules began to be built with toothed gearing and metal rollers. In other cases, inventors added drums and used parallel scrolling to generate smoother acceleration and deceleration. To install the newest textile technology at the Twist Mill, the decision was made to expand the building to the south in the late 1790s, with the extension comprising a seven-storey mule-spinning block. The early success of Salford Twist Mill prompted the construction of a third mill, added to the north-west of the original structure.

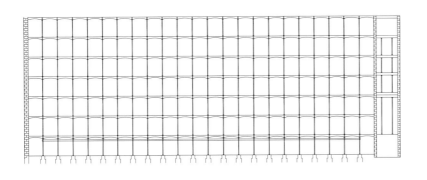

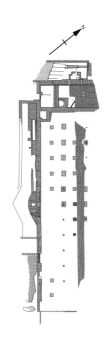

Recreation of drawing by Boulton & Watt of the new mill dating to 1805, showing parabolic beams alongside the remains uncovered during excavation (© Salford Archaeology)

At this time, mills were built with wooden beams and columns that were a constant fire hazard. Salford Twist Mill was one of the first industrial buildings to use two rows of cast-iron columns carrying cast-iron beams to support brick-vaulted ceilings. The iron components for this innovative structural frame were supplied by the leading engineering firm of Boulton & Watt in Birmingham. Drawings in the Boulton & Watt collection held in Birmingham City Library show the mill to have been seven storeys in height, including an attic and basement, each storey forming a room 63m long by 13m wide. The overall external dimensions, including the engine house, were 73m by 14m. The footprint of the new mill of 1799–1801 was targeted as part of the Phase 3 excavation in 2016, revealing 42m by 11m of the original mill building with a 27m by 3m external annexe to the south-west.

Aerial view of the Salford Twist Mill excavated in 2016 (© Salford Archaeology)

The pioneering design of the cast-iron framing is attributed to George Lee, an active partner in the Salford Twist Mill Company. The walls of the mill were completed up to the level of the first tier of beams during 1799, but progress thereafter appears to have been very slow until June 1800. The assembled iron frame was completed early in 1801 when at Lee's request William Creighton, one of Boulton & Watt's draughtsmen, made a perspective drawing of the columns and beams before the brick vaulting was added. The new construction technique

Original convex-based column in situ *on concave column base (© Salford Archaeology)*

was highly innovative and was designed when iron-frame construction was in its infancy. The iron columns were dual-purpose and were also intended to heat the building. Each column took the form of a hollow cylinder in place of a cruciform cross-section, allowing steam to pass through. In 1802, Boulton & Watt took their very first order for heating apparatus and supplied it to Salford Twist Mill. As a result, the mill was the first structure to use hollow support columns to transfer steam for heating.

The ground-floor arches were built in March of 1801, but in July the foundations of a column failed, causing part of the mill to collapse and resulting in one fatality. A note on a drawing in the Boulton & Watt collection records 'solid stone built after the failure of July 27, 1801'. Archaeological evidence pertaining to the early accident was uncovered during the excavation comprising a levelling layer of crushed sandstone overlying natural sandstone. The levelling layer had been deposited to a depth of 1.6m at the north-west and to 2.1m in the centre of the main mill; this became deeper as the bedrock descended towards the river. The levelling of the site fits with an historical account that refers to 'the filling in with 4½ feet of stonework of a space extending from bedrock to the foundations' to reinforce the structure following the fatality. Above the stone levelling material was a 0.2m thick layer of mixed sandstone and brick fragments, onto which a series of supporting stone bases were laid.

The Boulton & Watt plan shows the original layout of two rows of iron columns positioned to support the building and fireproof the structure. During the excavation, the bases for five rows of columns were uncovered. The original two sets of columns had 81cm by 93cm rectangular stone bases, with a 51cm square cast-iron base inserted above. The cast-iron base was chamfered up to 5cm high above a 23cm square pad for the column. Within the centre of the pad was a shallow 25cm diameter concave 'pocket' into which the column was placed. The columns themselves were 16.5cm in diameter and at the base had a 23cm diameter solid iron 'foot' with a convex base. The original layout of the columns was redesigned, possibly during the construction work after the failure of the column in July 1801, and the columns were reinforced with much more substantial bases consisting of alternate layers of brick and stone blocks down to bedrock.

Rows of column bases excavated in the basement of Salford Twist Mill

Three further rows of columns were added at a slightly later date, comprising substantial brick bases to bedrock, 2.1m in depth, with 66cm square and 4cm thick stone bases on top. On these sat 45cm square and 3cm thick cast-iron column base each with a 10cm diameter circular recess for the bottom of the column with a 3.6cm wide straight flange at either side. The columns on these bases were different to the original two rows, having a cruciform-shaped foot with two slots for the flanges on the column base.

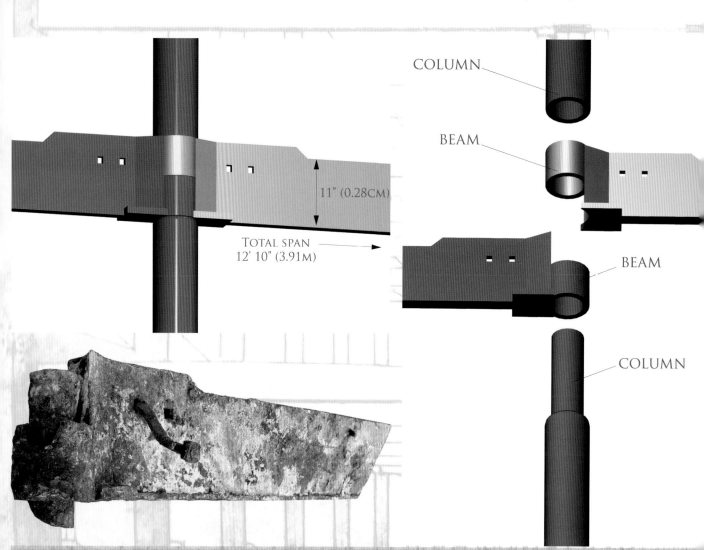

COLUMN

BEAM

BEAM

COLUMN

11" (0.28CM)

TOTAL SPAN
12' 10" (3.91M)

How the beams in the mill would have slotted together. According to the design drawings produced by Boulton & Watt in July / August 1799, the beams were to be of 12ft 10in span (3.91m) with a depth of 11in (0.28m) (© Salford Archaeology)

A unique assemblage of cast-iron artefacts was recovered from the excavation, representing a rare survival of fabric associated with the earliest iron-framed building within the region. Items identified were primarily columns and ceiling beams relating to the original iron frame of Salford Twist Mill. The assemblage therefore represents an invaluable resource in the understanding of the method of construction of this highly significant structure.

Before the crushed sandstone levelling was laid to support the new mill, the ground was excavated down to bedrock. The historic excavation avoided disturbing an *in-situ* column, an early flue and a possible flywheel pit at the north-west end of the mill. The flywheel pit and early flue were constructed from hand-made bricks and lime mortar, consistent with a late 18th- or early 19th-century date. The remains are likely to have been associated with the mill's original steam engine, while the early flue was connected to a chimney. Boulton & Watt drawings dating to 1801 show that a new engine house was built in an annexe at the northern part of the main mill building, housing a 60hp steam engine.

Flywheel pit and 19th-century flue
(© Salford Archaeology)

By the end of 1801 the mill was complete, and most of the machinery had been installed by April 1802. Within the north-west annexe were the remains of an engine bed, a bearing box built into the north-west external wall and a series of cast-iron steam pipes, one of which had a high-pressure collar. One of the earliest features within the room was a partially covered circular well, which would have provided a supply of water, likely associated with condensing for the engine. Several phases of development were evident

Circular well situated in the north-west annexe
(© Salford Archaeology)

within the building, including the blocking of the apertures that acted as conduits for the cast-iron pipes with hand-made bricks and black ash mortar consistent with a post-1860 date, presumably associated with the mill's conversion into a bonded warehouse.

George Lee, one of the founding partners of the Salford Twist Co, took advantage of the great inventions that distinguished the late 18th century and successfully applied them to the new mill, renamed in 1804 as Phillips & Lee. Lee's passion for science, and friendship with other ambitious engineers, led to Salford Twist Mill becoming the first steam-powered mill in Salford and the first iron-framed, 'fireproof' structure in the region. In 1806, a second engineering feat was accomplished when the mill reputedly became the first in the world to have been lit by gas.

From before Roman times until the early 19th century, artificial sources of light remained unchanged, consisting of various types of oil lamps and candles, which were taxed until 1831 and could only be afforded by the wealthy. The only source of artificial light available for working-class people was the light of a fire or from rushlamps. Few advances in lighting technology meant that it was impractical to light large spaces after dark, confining activities to daylight hours until the late 18th century. In domestic-based industries, artificial light was too poor to enable craftsmen to work at night and in most cases, craft guilds prohibited their members from working before sunrise or after sunset.

By the end of the 18th century, attitudes towards working during the hours of dark were changed irreversibly by the rise of the factory-based system. The world's first successful water-powered cotton mill was opened in 1771 by Richard Arkwright in Cromford, Derbyshire.

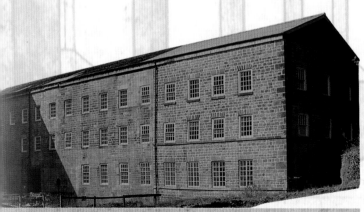

The remaining three storeys of the original Cromford Mill

Almost immediately after the mill was opened, it began to operate 24 hours a day, lit at night by a huge quantity of candles and oil lamps. The sight of the cotton mill lit up at night was unprecedented and drew a huge amount of attention. Nevertheless, the cost and fire risk associated with lighting mills by candle or oil lamps was problematic. A solution that would transform lighting technology came during experiments into the flammability of coal gas.

The flammability of escaping natural gases from coal or oil shale beds was first written about in 1667 in a paper to the Royal Society by Thomas Shirley named 'A Description of a Well and Earth in Lancashire taking Fire, by a Candle approaching to it'. John Clayton, a vicar from Wakefield, continued Shirley's work and in 1684 he excavated the base of the spring to find coal located 18 inches beneath the surface. The gas escaping from the coal measures was flammable and led to Clayton producing the earliest report on the distillation of coal in an open retort to produce a flammable gas. Experiments by other enthusiasts and scientists continued, and in 1726 Dr Stephen Hale was the first person to procure a flammable fluid from the distillation of coal, although scientists overlooked the usefulness of the liquid. It was not until 1790, when William Murdoch began experimenting with flammable gases, that its full potential was recognised.

William Murdoch (1754–1839)

Murdoch, an employee of Boulton & Watt, was specifically conducting experiments to see which gas would be most suitable for fuelling lamps. Coal gas undoubtedly produced the brightest flame and Murdoch began installing gas lighting in his house in Cornwall, completed by 1792. The gas was produced by distillation of coal, and was stored and transported through tubes to illuminate gas lamps. It was not until Gregory Watt (James Watt's son) visited Paris and saw the work of rival Philppe Lebon that Murdoch's employers began to fully support his research, eventually investing £5000 in Murdoch's experiments into the process of coal gas manufacture for commercial purposes.

In 1802, Murdoch lit the exterior of Boulton & Watt's Soho Foundry in Birmingham to celebrate the Peace of Amiens. The illumination was the first public exhibition of gas lighting and attracted much interest. Murdoch and his assistant Samuel Clegg continued experiments into making gas and designing retorts before Clegg resigned in 1805 to establish his own firm, eventually patenting his own inventions that helped to develop the gas industry.

Murdoch's original circular gasometer at the Soho gas plant
(Courtesy of Boulton & Watt Collection, Birmingham)

Meanwhile, George Lee began to show an interest in the new technology. His interest may have been motivated by an insurance quote that was one third of the previous cost if Salford Twist Mill was converted to gas lighting. Lee arranged for gas lighting to be trialled in his house in 1804 before deciding to install it in his factory. A letter from Phillips & Lee dated 19th July 1803 is held in the Boulton & Watt archive. The date of the letter and its contents imply that preparations for the gas works were already underway. The letter seems to provide Boulton & Watt with an update on progress at the mill, highlighting that Phillips & Lee had prepared the gasometer pits and house and required parts ordering for seating the bottom of the retorts and constructing fireplaces associated with heating the retorts.

In 1805, Boulton & Watt supplied the first retorts to Salford Twist Mill, which were similar to those that Murdoch used for his experiments at Soho and consisted of a vertical cylindrical vessel with a single door on the top. The gas-making plant was officially commissioned on 1st January 1806, representing Boulton & Watt's first commercial production of gas-making plant. In 1808, Murdoch presented a paper to the Royal Society that described the application of coal gas to the property of Messrs. Phillips & Lee at Salford Twist Mill. The gas plant comprised eight holders housed in a rectangular building, and a retort. This basic design served as the prototype for larger plants built in other cities in Britain. The mill itself would have been the first to be lit by this technique, although Samuel Clegg claimed to have installed plant two weeks prior to Murdoch at Willow Hall Mill in Halifax, West Yorkshire. Nevertheless, the publicity surrounding the use of gas at the Salford Twist Mill prompted a surge in orders for gas plant, and Murdoch claimed that the annual lighting bill at Salford Twist Mill had been reduced from £2000 using candles to £600.

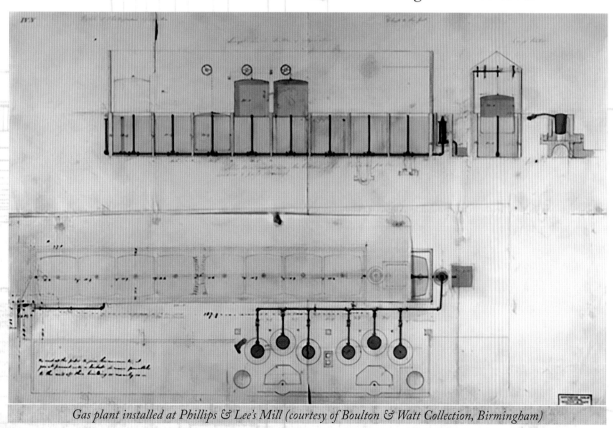

Gas plant installed at Phillips & Lee's Mill (courtesy of Boulton & Watt Collection, Birmingham)

Between 1806 and 1811, the average cost for the installation of a gas works was approximately £1088, yet the cost for the plant at the Salford Twist Mill was £4104. The excessive sum paid by Phillips & Lee was partly a result of having a huge quantity of lights installed, but they also presumably paid a premium as Boulton & Watt's first customer. Salford Twist Mill was lit with 550 cockspur and 300 Argand lights, equivalent to approximately 3725 candles. The number of lights at the Twist Mill was extravagant; comparisons with mills of a similar size suggest that between 1000 and 2200 candle equivalents were sufficient. After gas lighting was installed at Salford Twist Mill, plans to install 4200 lamps at McConnell & Kennedy's large mill complex in Ancoats were reduced to 2200, implying that fewer lights were required than expected initially.

The gas plant was situated on the south-west side of the mill close to the River Irwell. This is depicted on the Ordnance Survey map of 1851, while a plan of 1808 shows a long range in the same location. This area lay outside the Chapel Wharf development zone and so was not included in the archaeological investigations carried out on the site, but does play a significant role in the history of the mill and development of the Chapel Wharf area.

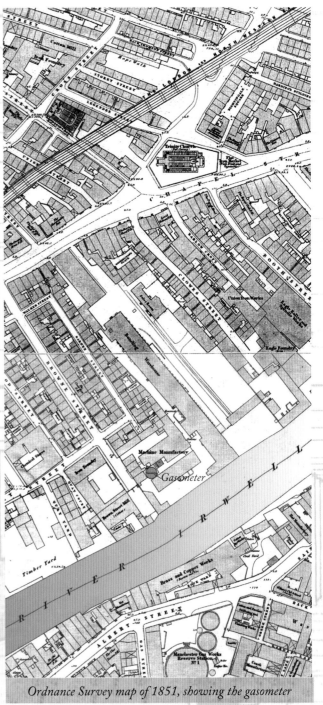

Ordnance Survey map of 1851, showing the gasometer

The gas plant not only lit the mill but also supplied gas to several lights on Chapel Street, making this the earliest street in the world known to have been lit by gas. Public lighting had previously been non-existent, and from the 15th century had relied on residents leaving a candle to hang outside their homes between Hallowtide (31st October) and Candlemasse (2nd February).

Gas works sprang up around the country during the 19th century, particularly in industrial towns where demand was greater, and by 1826 only two towns in Britain with a population over 10,000 did not have at least one gas company. In the most part, the cost and technical demands of gas production soon favoured large, centralised works over small private ones, like that at Salford Twist Mill. In Salford, in 1819, a group of local businessmen named Thomas Appleby, Richard Bain, Edward Fisher and a Mr Clay built one of the earliest public gas works in the region. This was situated on Clowes Street, adjacent to Salford Twist Mill, and was in operation by the autumn of 1820.

In 1830, an Act of Parliament allowed the Salford Police Commissioners to purchase the works on Clowes Street. The position of the Clowes Street gas works is shown on Swire's map of 1824 and Bancks & Co's map of 1831. By 1836 a new gas works in Lamb Lane, later known as Bloom Street, replaced the gas works at Clowes Street, which went out of use by the 1840s. In 1844 a Charter of Incorporation was granted to the town and gas works came under the control of Salford Corporation's Gas Committee. Gas production expanded and the growth in the number of gas companies continued until the industry was nationalised in 1948–49.

Gas light along Chapel Street (courtesy of Manchester Local Image Collection)

A labyrinth of streets surrounded the Twist Mill and its adjacent gas plant. The new streets were laid as masses of people began to migrate from the countryside to industrial towns to seek employment opportunities in the new factories. In turn, this caused Salford to expand further as huge numbers of houses were built to accommodate the influx of workers near their places of work.

The population of Salford rocketed from 4756 inhabitants in 1773 to 12,000 in 1812. Private developers saw this as an opportunity to exploit the working population by building low-quality terraced and back-to-back dwellings. These were built quickly and cheaply, with developers making economies wherever possible. The economical use of building materials is reflected in the archaeological record. Usually, the external walls were two bricks wide, while

An example of houses built on a small court in Salford; photo taken in 1890 (courtesy of Digital Salford)

single-skin walls were used for partitions. Archaeological excavations at Chapel Wharf revealed that this construction technique was used to build workers' houses at Clowes Street, although one dwelling was bound by single-skin walls. Contemporary accounts by social commentator and philanthropist Freidrick Engels imply that this was not unusual as he also records dwellings 'whose outer walls were but one-half brick thick, the bricks lying not sidewise but lengthwise, their narrow ends touching'. Engels also notes that 'the average construction of Salford is in this respect much worse than that of Manchester, and so, too, in respect to cleanliness'.

Green's map of 1787–94 shows that the entire Chapel Wharf area had been developed, with domestic dwellings lining a new grid of streets named Barlow's Croft, Clowes Street, Brown Street, Garden Street, Walker Street and Chapel Street. The construction cut for the earliest surviving structures at Clowes Street had been dug through a layer of garden or plough soil containing 16th- to 18th-century pottery.

Building 2 with alleyway in the foreground
(© University of Manchester Archaeological Unit)

Building 1 measured 5m by 5m and was demarcated by one-brick wide walls. A sandstone door jamb indicated the entrance into the building via an alleyway that ran north-east/south-west between building 1 and an early 19th-century cellar. The building next door had a similar-sized footprint, measuring 5.5m by 5m, but was bound by single-skin walls and had been divided into three rooms. The largest room measured 4m by 2.8m and included a fireplace and a hand-made brick drain raised above a floor of hand-made bricks.

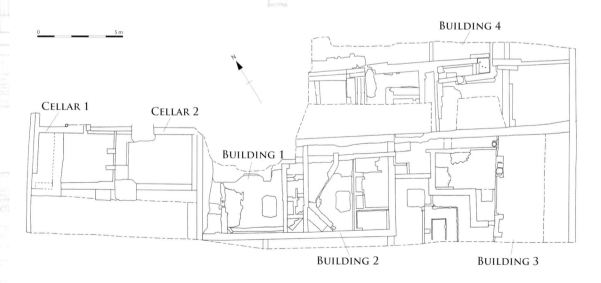

Plan of Clowes Street excavation, Phase 2, 2007 (© University of Manchester Archaeological Unit)

With elements of the workforce receiving low wages, together with the severe housing shortage, multiple-occupancy dwellings and cellars occupied by entire families were common in certain parts of Salford. Overcrowding exacerbated living conditions in dwellings that already lacked adequate space, light, ventilation and proper drainage. In addition, privies and water supplies were shared with multiple households, causing poor health and hygiene. The Ordnance Survey map

Arch chamber in cellar 2 (© University of Manchester Archaeological Unit)

of 1848 shows two water taps that served 41 dwellings in the area, most of which were probably overcrowded. Inevitably, these dire circumstances led to chronic social deprivation, poverty and high mortality rates within the working districts of Salford.

At Clowes Street, the remains of two basements of 19th-century tenements were uncovered alongside the 18th-century workers' houses. An interior wall, one brick wide divided the two cellared buildings. The first cellar had an intact fireplace built against an external wall of hand-made bricks. The second cellar was better preserved than the adjacent building and had the remnants of a barrel-vaulted ceiling and a floor of hand-made bricks. A small 0.74m deep half-arched chamber of unknown function was also evident within the cellar, as well as the ghost of two buttresses that presumably demarcated a fireplace. The inclusion of a fireplace in each cellar implies that they were both used as living accommodation.

Census returns show that many of the dwellings along Clowes Street were multiple-occupancy with two families and several lodgers living in most, averaging almost nine people per household. One of the most overcrowded dwellings was number 14 Clowes Street, recorded in the census of 1851, where four families, extended family members and lodgers, totalling 16 residents, plus six visitors, shared the dwelling. The youngest worker living at the address was 11-year-old Ellen Leatherbarrow, who worked as a servant. The 1881 census paints a similar picture and records the number of rooms let to individual families. At number 8 Clowes Street, Sarah Leatherbarrow and her niece rented one room at the property, while three more rooms were each let to three other families, suggesting that the cellar may have provided living space.

Some of the worst housing at Chapel Wharf was located on the small courts behind the main streets along Lowe's, Dan, Alsop's, Collin's, Broadhead's, Fullerton's and Williamson's courts. The houses built on these courts were typically two-storey high, single-depth, back-to-back dwellings. This type of dwelling was built as cheaply as possible, sharing three party walls with the neighbouring houses. The only windows and doors were located at the front of the building, so ventilation and light were limited. The census returns imply that throughout the 19th century not all of the back-to-backs were inhabited. On both Alsop's Court and Fullerton's Court, half of the houses were vacant. Although there was a housing shortage, it was common for houses to stand empty. At this time, the population was fairly transient and so very few families are listed at the same address in concurrent censuses.

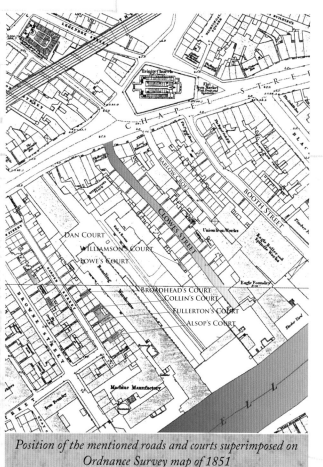

Position of the mentioned roads and courts superimposed on Ordnance Survey map of 1851

Growing concerns about sanitation and living conditions sparked philanthropists and pressure groups such as the Manchester and Salford Sanitary Association to campaign for social and housing reform. In March 1840, the government launched a public health inquiry to investigate the scale of overcrowding and disease among the working population, and recognised that the dwellings in these courts were unsuitable. Gradually legislation was introduced to improve appalling living conditions. An account from the early 1840s states that 'if, in Manchester, the policeforce, from time to time, every six or ten years, makes a raid upon the working people's districts, closes the worst dwellings, and causes the filthiest spots in these Augean stables to be cleansed, in Salford it seems to have done absolutely nothing. The narrow side lanes and courts of Chapel Street, Greengate, and Gravel Lane have certainly never been cleansed since they were built'.

Three shared privies in a Salford court, taken in the 1890s (courtesy of Digital Salford)

Further statutory measures were introduced in 1853, with a local bye-law, which attempted to ban cellar dwellings, resulting in a gradual decline in the number of inhabited cellars. Following the Public Health Act of 1875, local governments banned the construction of new back-to-back

An example of back-to-back dwellings in Pendlebury (courtesy of Digital Salford)

houses, which were replaced by bye-law terraced houses. Evidence for improvements at Chapel Wharf includes the conversion of back-to-backs on Walker Street into through houses by 1891 and the demolition of a single dwelling on Broadhead's Court, presumably to install privies. Elsewhere on the site there were very few improvements, and at least six plots of back-to-back dwellings were inhabited until the turn of the century.

Concealing the low-quality housing built on the streets to the rear of Chapel Street was an almost unbroken series of shops, small workshops and public houses. These commercial buildings occupied a much larger footprint and were better built, often comprising three-storey buildings with a cellar. The Georgian-period dwellings along Chapel Street within the Chapel Wharf area were first captured on Green's map of 1787–94, located opposite Sacred Trinity Church and close to the Flat Iron Market.

Salford Flat Iron Market; photo taken in 1889, with view of a row of houses along Church Street between Booth Street and Barlow's Croft (courtesy of Manchester Local Image Collection)

In 1841 and 1851, single families averaging five people per household occupied the properties along Chapel Street. Trade directories dating to 1850 record shopkeepers, greengrocers, hairdressers, bakers, butchers, confectioners and tobacconists operating small, family-run businesses from the rooms that fronted Chapel Street. Some of these businesses generated enough surplus money to employ one or more servants. In total, nine out of the 16 dwellings within the Chapel Wharf area employed servants in 1861. One of the most successful businesses was

93–99 Chapel Street in 1905. The tall building is on the corner of Clowes Street (courtesy of Digital Salford)

run by Ebenezer Starmer, a shoemaker, living at 93–99 Chapel Street, who employed six men and five women, and had two servants to run the household.

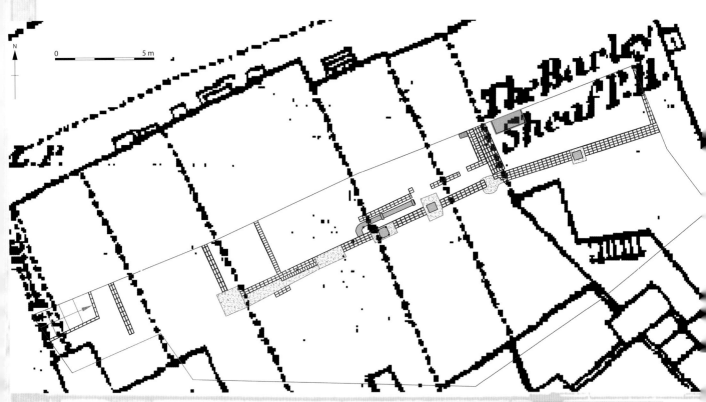

Phase 3 excavation results overlain on OS map of 1850 (© Salford Archaeology)

The footprints of properties along Chapel Street were targeted during the third phase of excavation in 2016. The fragmentary remains of a row of terraced properties were discovered in the north-west part of the site. The fabric of the structures comprised hand-made bricks and lime mortar, consistent with a late 18th- to early 19th-century date. Within the south-west part of the excavation were the remains of a room that contained an internal quarter-turn staircase. The staircase, which had a stone tread, was built against a partially exposed hand-made brick wall. Comparisons between the georectified survey and historic mapping suggest that the staircase was situated within the second from the end-of-row terrace at number 105/95 Chapel Street. In the 1850s, a local man named William Holmes lived at this address with his family, and ran a tobacconist from the dwelling. As the century progressed, the community became more diverse, and in the 1860s Gerson Marks, a Prussian subject (naturalised), and his wife Elizabeth, who was also Prussian, moved to the address and worked as watchmakers and tobacconists.

A one-brick wide partition wall was situated to the north-east of the staircase. The wall was identified as a partition when its surveyed position was superimposed onto historic mapping, confirming the notion that houses on Chapel Street were better built than those along Clowes Street which, in comparison, had been divided by a half-brick-wide wall.

Remains of a cellar at 99/95 Chapel Street, 2016 (©Salford Archaeology)

The remains of the only surviving intact cellar at 99/95 Chapel Street were situated to the north-east of the partition wall. Two additional one-brick-wide walls defined the cellar. The total area of the room was not exposed, but the floor surface had been paved with flagstones. Towards the base of the north-east wall were the remains of a 2.4m-wide arch. The arch survived up to 1.1m high and had been blocked with hand-made bricks. Presumably, the arch was built as a stress-relieving structure.

Junction of Booth Street and Chapel Street, 1985; see on p35 for orientation (courtesy of Digital Salford)

Shops along Chapel Street served the surrounding neighbourhood for the entire 19th century. By the 20th century, the area was in decline, and parts of Chapel Wharf were decimated by bombing in the Second World War. Despite this, some properties continued to function as shops throughout the late 20th century.

The Lord Nelson in 1985, on the corner of Barlow's Croft and next to 93 Chapel Street (courtesy of Digital Salford)

Archaeological excavations along Clowes Street and Barlow's Croft in 2007 revealed that not all of the dwellings retained their domestic function. Some of the properties appear to have been converted into small workshops by knocking through the walls of multiple houses.

Building 3 with possible workshop bench bases, 2007 (© University of Manchester Archaeological Unit)

Building 3 measured 6.2m by 5m and probably represented the remains of a late 18th-century workshop, presumably built to accommodate a cottage industry. The building had a cellar with a floor surface of hand-made bricks. Within the cellar, a rectangular brick-built structure covered with cast-iron plates was interpreted as a fixture used to lift items in and out of the cellar. Next to the cellar, in another room of the workshop, a structure interpreted as a base for workshop tables was discovered.

Behind buildings 2 and 3, fronting Barlow's Croft, were the remains of a late 18th-early 19th-century factory, shown on the OS map of 1891 as a gum and starch factory. A similar footprint of the factory is shown on the earlier OS town plan of 1850. The ground beneath the factory had been levelled with a layer of mixed very compact dark loam with abundant crushed brick, stone, slate and cinders before its construction. Four hand-made brick walls with cobbled foundations defined the building. The surface of the building had a partially surviving hand-made brick floor, which overlay an earlier cobbled surface. Slater's trade directory of 1895 records Smith & Kersley as gum and starch manufacturers, and Goad's insurance plan of 1893 names the site as Albion Works.

Evidence was found of several attempts to reinforce the structure. In addition, the remains of an early flue and square chimney base and three holding-down bolts survived within the factory. The presence of the holding-down bolts may indicate the position of ovens or mechanical plant listed on Goad's insurance plan. The flue and chimney, and the structural reinforcements, are likely also associated with upgrading an earlier property to accommodate the ovens.

Chimney and flue, 2007 (© University of Manchester Archaeological Unit)

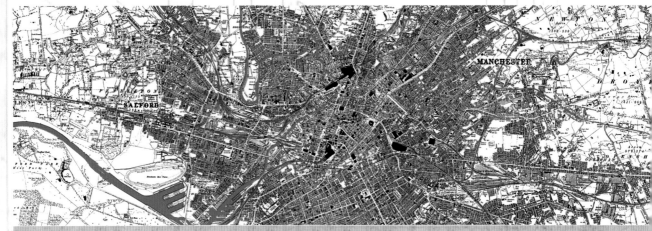

Ordnance Survey county plan of 1896, showing the railways (red) and watercourses (blue) that ran through Manchester and Salford at the time and were key in the transportation of materials and goods

The transportation of materials and goods was of utmost importance, and improvements to transport routes went hand-in-hand with the growth of industry. The various mills and factories at Chapel Wharf were served by the canalised River Irwell, providing a navigable route to the Port of Liverpool. Additionally, the Manchester Bolton & Bury Canal facilitated the economical transportation of coal from the collieries situated to the north of Salford.

The advent of the railways and the exponential growth of the railway network across the country meant that freight and passengers could be transported on an unprecedented scale. By 1838, the mills had access to the newly established Manchester & Bolton Railway, later incorporated into the Lancashire & Yorkshire Railway. The viaduct for the new railway line traversed residential areas, demolishing pockets of workers' houses to the south-west of Chapel Wharf.

Constructing the Manchester ship canal, 1890 (courtesy of Digital Salford)

Further advances in transport came with the opening of the Manchester Ship Canal in 1894, which turned Manchester and Salford into land-locked ports that could handle ocean-going vessels. The construction of this canal was intended to bypass the Port of Liverpool, and shortly after its opening, the Port of Manchester became the third busiest port in Britain, despite being 40 miles from the coast.

Storage of manufactured goods was another important factor, and many warehouses were built adjacent to factories and transport links. During the initial phase of industrialisation, merchants stored goods manufactured in weavers' cottages

Alcohol stored in a warehouse in Salford in 1904 (courtesy of Digital Salford)

in their own homes, or bought neighbouring properties to use as warehouse space. The rapid growth of industrialisation meant that items were mass-produced and required large storage facilities in purpose-built warehouses.

During the 18th century, a rise in the number of imported commodities from the British Empire increased the need for warehouse space at ports. Payments on imported items were expensive and regulations required that the payment of duties had to be made at the time of importation, or a bond with security for future payment was given to the revenue authorities. This system was inefficient, and the large amount of capital required for the importation of more heavily taxed items, such as tobacco and alcohol, prevented the development of competition. Robert Walpole proposed an excise scheme for the warehousing of tobacco and wine in 1733. However, this was unpopular with merchants and was not adopted into British law until 1803. The new system allowed imported dutiable goods, such as spirits or tobacco, to be stored in customs-controlled bonded warehouses before payment of the duty. Most bonded warehouses had few windows, usually barred, and a single heavy entranceway to minimise the risk of the high-value goods being burgled.

In 1836 the Salford Twist Mill went out of use as a factory, and it was taken over by the Manchester Bonded Warehouse Company in the early 1840s. An article from the *Chester Chronicle* dating to 28th February 1845 advertises the Manchester Bonded Warehouse Company. The article reveals that the company received their deed of registration according to the Manchester Bonding Act of 'last season' and was ready to receive goods 'in bond'. Goods that are either about to or have already entered the warehouse are listed and include 3072 bales of cotton, 1438 chests of tea, 413 bales of madder roots (otherwise known as dyer's madder), 83 bags of yellow berries, 62 bags of coffee, 13 (illegible) of coffee, 8 hogsheads of sugar, 260 bags of sugar and 28 bales of silk. The content of the advert gives an insight into the initial success of the company and the variety of products stored in the warehouse.

Aerial view of the Bonded Warehouse in the 1930s, showing Sacred Trinity Church and Blackfriars Bridge (© Britain from Above and Historic England)

One of the first commodities to be sold from the bonded warehouse saleroom was chests of tea, advertised in the *Lancashire General Advertiser* of 29th March 1845, which also praises the new bonding system. The associated saleroom is labelled on the OS map of 1851 and is situated north-east of the bonded warehouse. Throughout the 1840s, the bonded warehouse increasingly stored and sold sugar imported from Bengal and Barbados.

In 1861, the Commissioner of Customs granted Manchester Bonded Warehouse Company Limited the privilege of bottling wines and spirits. The processing of the alcohol was undertaken in specific rooms. Alcohol and other goods stored in the warehouse could undergo manipulation by repackaging, cleaning, sorting or changing their condition, using processes that made the products fit for market. A huge quantity of early 20th-century wine, brandy, dry gin, whisky, cognac and champagne bottles were recovered from the basement of the warehouse during the 2016 excavation.

Bottled wine and spirits recovered from the 2016 excavation

In 1875, the fifth floor of the warehouse was leased to Carr, Render & Co, corn and flour merchants. Shortly after their arrival, in 1877, two of the upper floors of the warehouse collapsed and the tenants requested to be released from their contract. Manchester Bonded Warehouse Company Limited began an appeal to obtain costs amounting to £360 for accruing rent, but the appeal was dismissed and is recorded in the *Manchester Evening News* on 26th November 1883. The upper floors of the warehouse were subsequently rebuilt.

Reports from *The Yorkshire Post* and *Leeds Intelligencer* record that the net profit of Manchester Bonded Warehouse in 1920 was £8606.

In-situ *bottles during the 2016 excavation*

Air raids during the Second World War in 1939 drastically changed the appearance of Manchester and Salford when it became a target for a German bombing campaign, carried out by the Luftwaffe. Airstrikes targeted Britain's seaports together with industrial towns and cities such as Birmingham, Belfast, Coventry, Glasgow, Liverpool, Manchester and Sheffield. Raids began on London towards the end of the Battle of Britain in September 1940 targeting factories, public utilities and food stock. To avoid counter-attacks by the RAF, the Luftwaffe ceased daylight operations and began a night bombing campaign from October 1940. The air strikes became known as 'The Blitz', a term coined by the British press, derived from the German word for lighting.

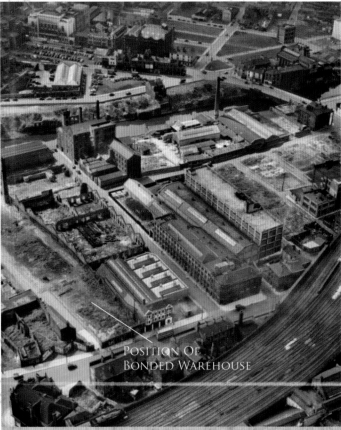

Area of bombed industrial buildings off Chapel Street including the Bonded Warehouse, 1950 (© Britain from Above)

The Luftwaffe developed their tactics and from the autumn of 1940 other industrial cities were under attack. Manchester was an important inland sea port and industrial city, while Trafford Park in neighbouring Stretford was an important centre for war production. Major raids occurred on Sunday 22nd and Monday 23rd December, known as the Christmas Blitz. The Luftwaffe intentionally bombed cities on consecutive nights to inflict maximum disruption and destruction. On the first night of raids, 272 tons of high explosive bombs were dropped. The following night another 195 tons of high explosives hit the city. Almost 2000 incendiaries were also dropped on the city across the two nights.

Airstrikes during the Christmas Blitz hit three known locations along or in the vicinity of Chapel Street, including Salford Royal Hospital, Bloom Street and Blackfriars Street. It is likely that the Bonded Warehouse was hit during the Christmas raid, but it is very unlikely that the building was intentionally targeted.

A Second World War German aerial incendiary bomb of the type that destroyed the Twist Mill

Whilst it contained a large quantity of consumable items and was sited within a complex of industrial buildings, it is more probable that it was hit during airstrikes on Manchester Exchange railway station. Major railway routes into the city were targeted to disrupt supply lines and block routes. Exchange Station was no exception and was showered with high explosives and incendiary bombs during the Christmas Blitz. Incendiary bombs caused around 600 fires. Some of the worst affected buildings were commercial and warehouse buildings, many of which burnt to the ground while the majority of Manchester's firefighters were helping to extinguish fires caused by raids in Liverpool.

Smaller bombardments took place in June 1941, when the worst of the Blitz was thought to be over. During this raid, Salford Royal Hospital on Chapel Street was hit again, killing 14 nurses. It is also possible that the Bonded Warehouse was hit during this raid.

Spirits within the basement of the warehouse were partially protected from the fire, and, during the excavation, were discovered in burnt wooden crates. Several bottles of champagne were even found with their contents and corks intact. Twelve bottles of port were recovered. Paper labels, with visible writing on them, were still attached to some of the bottles. Although only parts were readable, the words 'Vinho', meaning wine, 'Registrada' and 'exposicao', meaning exhibition, could be made out. Many of the glass bottles were melted and misshapen from the intense heat of the fire caused by incendiary bombs.

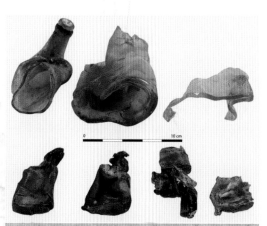

Bottles of spirits melted out of shape by the high temperatures of the burning incendiary bombs

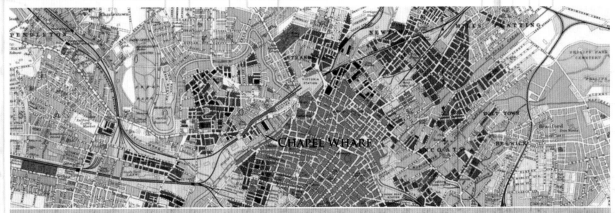

J R Corbett's map showing housing conditions in Manchester and Salford, 1904. Dwellings regarded as 'slum properties' are shaded in dark brown. The Chapel Wharf area is shown to have very few houses

Friedrich Engels painted a bleak picture of the working people's living conditions in the 1830s, when private developers were throwing up back-to-back houses and the poorest families were occupying cold, dark and dank cellar dwellings. Although some steps were taken in Manchester and Salford to tackle appalling housing conditions through local legislation, progress was slow, and at the turn of the 20th century a considerable number of homes remained substandard. The persistent housing problem in Manchester and Salford is best illustrated in a map compiled by J R Corbett for Thomas Marr's book, which drew on the work of members of the Citizens' Association for the Improvement of the Unwholesome Dwellings and Surroundings of the People.

The map shows the extent of 'slum' areas at the turn of the century, despite the clearance of swathes of back-to-back housing. By 1904, buildings at Chapel Wharf were characterised by a mixture of warehouses, and a block of back-to-backs, which continued to be inhabited, on Garden Street. Just before the outbreak of the First World War, most of these properties had been cleared and were replaced by warehouses. A survey undertaken in 1931, reported that Salford still had some of the worst housing in the country. By 1933, slum clearance was underway and some Georgian terraces were replaced by tower blocks in the 1960s and '70s.

Clearance in the Trinity area of Salford, to the south west of Chapel Wharf, in 1955

Rising unemployment during the Great Depression of the 1920s and '30s hit Salford's economy hard. Industries were already struggling with foreign competition; by 1939 most of the collieries had closed and the textile industry was in decline. A lack of jobs, in an area formerly renowned for its abundance of industries, and the provision of new housing estates on the periphery of the city, led to population decline in the years following the Second World War.

The Ordnance Survey map of 1948 shows the scale of destruction on the industrial complex at Chapel Wharf. The former bonded warehouse is labelled as a ruin, together with Trinity House (a cotton waste warehouse), numbers 93–115 Chapel Street, a finishing works on the south-east side of the warehouse, and numerous factories and buildings along Clowes Street.

Aerial view of Chapel Street and Chapel Wharf in the second half of the 20th century (© Britain from Above)

From the mid-1950s Salford experienced large-scale clearance and housing redevelopment, and the Slum Clearance Compensation Act (1965) and the Housing Subsidies Act (1967) accelerated the transformation. New works and warehouses were rebuilt at Chapel Wharf, but by the end of the 20th century, these were deemed no longer fit for purpose. In the late 1990s and early 21st century, considerable investments were made in the Greengate and Chapel Street area to construct modern sustainable accommodation, and provide jobs and facilities for new and existing communities.

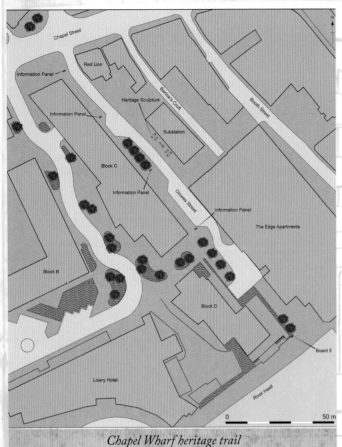

Chapel Wharf heritage trail

Dandara Limited delivered the development at Chapel Wharf, financed by Sir Robert McAlpine, comprising four apartment blocks with 995 apartments arranged over 22 storeys. The development is set in a prime location, within walking distance of Manchester's cultural district and the Spinningfields business quarter. A major part of the Chapel Wharf redevelopment included the opening of the five-star Lowry Hotel in 2001. The construction of the Lowry Hotel has attracted new visitors to the city and has created an abundance of jobs in the hospitality, administration and leisure sectors.

Development projects must consider known or suspected archaeological sites to safeguard any remains by sensitive planning or, when necessary, archaeological excavation and recording. Current planning policy also advises that the results from archaeological work are disseminated to the public in an appropriate format. Part of the programme of dissemination at Chapel Wharf agreed with GMAAS on behalf of Salford City Council involved the creation of a 'heritage trail', including five information panels situated on Clowes Street. The panels explain the history of Chapel Wharf and describe the archaeological excavations covered in this booklet. In addition to the information panels, a cast-iron sculpture has been erected on Clowes Street, formed from some of the columns that once supported the Salford Twist Mill.

Funding from Dandara Limited has provided Salford Archaeology with the relevant resources to produce this publication. This booklet presents an illustrated summary of the results gained from important archaeological excavations on a plot of land that was on the fringe of Salford's medieval core, and became the home of one of the most sophisticated and innovative industrial buildings in the world.

BACK-TO-BACK: a type of terraced house which shares three of four party walls with neighbouring houses.

BARREL VAULTED: a semi-cylindrical-shaped ceiling.

BURGAGE: a narrow plot of land within medieval and post-medieval towns that was rented to an individual.

COTTAGE INDUSTRY: a small-scale – usually manufacturing – business with producers working at home on their own equipment.

EARTHENWARE: clay that has been fired at a reasonably low temperature. Unless it is glazed, it is porous to liquids.

FLYWHEEL: a large wheel attached to a piston by a crank. Once the flywheel is set in motion, constant power is maintained and the action of alternating strokes from the piston is smoothed.

HP (HORSEPOWER): a unit of power. It was originally defined to allow the output of steam engines to be measured and compared with the power output of horses. The horsepower was widely adopted to measure the output of piston engines, electric motors and other machinery. Specific definitions vary, although that used most commonly equates one horsepower (1hp) to 735–746 watts.

RETORT: a closed tube, heated within a furnace, in which coal is baked to release coal gas.

RUSHLAMP: the dried pith of a rush plant, dipped in fat, which was burnt, serving as a source of artificial light.

SLIPWARE: pottery that has been dipped into a liquid clay, resulting in a shiny attractive finish.

SPINNING MULE: a machine for spinning cotton and other fibres, which was a hybrid of Arkwright's water frame and the spinning jenny. It was invented by Samuel Crompton in 1775–79, but despite there being over 4 million mules in operation by 1812, Crompton was unable to take out a patent on his invention and so received no royalties.

WATERFRAME: a spinning frame, able to spin many threads at a time, powered by a waterwheel. The spinning frame was patented by Richard Arkwright in 1769.

' Engels, F, 1845 *The Condition of the Working Class in England*, London

' Fletcher, K, 2020 *Salford Regeneration: The Archaeology of Living in the City*, Greater Manchester's Past Revealed, 27, Salford

' Fletcher, K, and Miller, I, 2022 *Douglas Green, Pendleton: The Archaeology of an Industrial Colony*, Greater Manchester's Past Revealed, 30, Salford

' Greenall, RL, 2000 *The Making of Victorian Salford*, Lancaster

' Gregory, R, and Miller, I, 2015 *Greengate: The Archaeology of Salford's Historic Core*, Greater Manchester's Past Revealed, 13, Lancaster

' Haslam, R, Proctor, J and Ridgeway, V, 2017 *Exchange Station, Greengate, Salford: The History and Archaeology of a Transformed Urban Landscape*, Greater Manchester's Past Revealed, 18, London

' Tann, J, 1970 *The Development of the Factory*, London

' Thomson, J, 2003 *The Scot Who Lit The World, The Story Of William Murdoch Inventor Of Gas Lighting*, privately published

Most of the historical maps used in this booklet can be found at Manchester Archives and Local Studies in Manchester Central Library, and at Salford Local History Library in Salford Museum and Art Gallery.

Copies of the detailed technical reports from the excavations by the University of Manchester Archaeological Unit, Oxford Archaeology North, and Salford Archaeology have been deposited with the Greater Manchester Historic Environment Record.

Publications in the *Greater Manchester's Past Revealed* series are available from GMAAS within the University of Salford, and digital copies of all the volumes published between 2010 and 2021 can be downloaded at https://gmaas.salford.ac.uk/publications/